Visit Bik

Copyright Stephen R. Wilson

Contents

1. Jesus Brings Lazarus Back to Life! ... 5
2. Mary Pours Perfume on Jesus ... 12
3. Palm Sunday – Jesus Rides into Jerusalem on a Donkey ... 15
4. Jesus Teaches His Disciples How to Serve One Another ... 19
5. Last Supper – Communion ... 25
6. Jesus is Arrested ... 33
7. Jesus Dies and Takes Away our Sins ... 42
8. The Real Meaning of the Easter Basket ... 49
9. Jesus is Raised! ... 53
10. The Empty Grave ... 57
11. On the Road to Emmaus ... 63
12. Jesus Appears to His Disciples ... 68
13. Jesus Forgives Peter ... 74
14. Jesus Gives His Disciples Their Mission and Promises to Always Be With Them ... 79
15. Jesus Goes Back Up to Heaven – The Ascension ... 82

Note: All Scripture quotations I've included are from the NIV, but feel free to use any translation you prefer.

Jesus' Death and Resurrection

Greetings, teachers! It's time for the end game of Jesus' life (or should I say, His first physical life) here on earth. Starting with the resurrection of Lazarus, we'll see how the Jewish and Roman leaders, and even some of His own disciples, turned against Jesus.

But that was all part of God's plan because Jesus' mission was to die in our place. And that wasn't the end of the story, of course. God brought Jesus back to life, and someday, Jesus will return and bring all of us back to life too!

Each of the 15 lessons in this volume has games, crafts, and other activities to help you teach the stories and to help the kids apply the message. I'm also including a list of resources you might want to add to the lessons to make them that much better.

Recommended Extras

You don't need anything extra to use the lessons. I will, however, provide some suggestions you might find helpful. You can use these resources in addition to or instead of the ideas I've provided.

Here are the resources I recommend for the entire series. I'll list story-specific resources at the end of each lesson or the beginning of each section.

The Complete Illustrated Children's Bible – for telling the stories with beautiful artwork and Biblical accuracy

The Beginner's Bible: Timeless Stories for Children – for telling the stories to younger children

Manga Comic Book: Messiah – for your classroom or church library

My Big Book of Bible Heroes Devotional – a devotional to recommend for families or older students

Jesus - To Eternity and Beyond (Discover 4 Yourself series) – in-depth Bible study book for older children based on John 17-21

Jesus Brings Lazarus Back to Life!

Use this children's Sunday School lesson to teach kids about the power of Jesus in raising Lazarus (and us) from the dead.

Needed: Bibles, drawing paper, crayons or colored pencils

Intro Activity: Acting It Out – Divide students into groups of two or three. Give them a few minutes to think of their skit. Then, have each group act out what they think happens when someone dies.

Lesson: (Note: Always give students the opportunity to answer the questions before you clarifying the teaching.)

(Read John 11:1-3.)

"Now a man named Lazarus was sick. He was from Bethany, the village of Mary and her sister Martha. (This Mary, whose brother Lazarus now lay sick, was the same one who poured perfume on the Lord and wiped His feet with her hair.) So the sisters sent word to Jesus, 'Lord, the one You love is sick.'"

Why do you think Mary and Martha sent a message to Jesus, telling Him that Lazarus is sick? (They believed that Jesus could help Lazarus get better by healing him.)

Do you think Jesus could heal Lazarus? (Yes.)

And Jesus can help us too when we're sick or have problems.

(Read John 11:4-7.)

"When He heard this, Jesus said, 'This sickness will not end in death. No, it is for God's glory so that God's Son may be glorified through it.' Now Jesus loved Martha and her sister and Lazarus. So when He heard that Lazarus was sick, He stayed where He was two more days, and then He said to His disciples, 'Let us go back to Judea.'"

Mary and Martha sent a message for Jesus to come to heal Lazarus. But did Jesus go to them right away? (No. He waited two days and then, He went to them.)

Why do you think Jesus didn't go to them right away?

(Read John 11:8-35.)

"'But Rabbi,' they said, 'a short while ago the Jews there tried to stone You, and yet You are going back?'

"Jesus answered, 'Are there not twelve hours of daylight? Anyone who walks in the daytime will not stumble, for they see by this world's light. It is when a person walks at night that they stumble, for they have no light.'

"After He had said this, He went on to tell them, 'Our friend Lazarus has fallen asleep; but I am going there to wake him up.'

"His disciples replied, 'Lord, if he sleeps, he will get better.' Jesus had been speaking of his death, but His disciples thought He meant natural sleep.

"So then He told them plainly, 'Lazarus is dead, and for your sake I am glad I was not there, so that you may believe. But let us go to him.'

"Then Thomas (also known as Didymus) said to the rest of the disciples, 'Let us also go, that we may die with Him.'

"On his arrival, Jesus found that Lazarus had already been in the tomb for four days. Now Bethany was less than two miles from Jerusalem, and many Jews had come to Martha and Mary to comfort them in the loss of their brother. When Martha heard that Jesus was coming, she went out to meet Him, but Mary stayed at home.

"'Lord,' Martha said to Jesus, 'if You had been here, my brother would not have died. But I know that even now God will give You whatever You ask.'

"Jesus said to her, 'Your brother will rise again.'

"Martha answered, 'I know he will rise again in the resurrection at the last day.'

"Jesus said to her, 'I am the resurrection and the life. The one who believes in Me will live, even though they die; and whoever lives by believing in Me will never die. Do you believe this?'

"'Yes, Lord,' she replied, 'I believe that you are the Messiah, the Son of God, who is to come into the world.'

"After she had said this, she went back and called her sister Mary aside. 'The Teacher is here,' she said, 'and is asking for you.' When Mary heard this, she got up quickly and went to Him. Now Jesus had not yet entered the village, but was still at the place where Martha had met Him. When the Jews who had been with Mary in the house, comforting her, noticed how quickly she got up and went out, they followed her, supposing she was going to the tomb to mourn there.

"When Mary reached the place where Jesus was and saw Him, she fell at His feet and said, 'Lord, if you had been here, my brother would not have died.'

'When Jesus saw her weeping, and the Jews who had come along with her also weeping, He was deeply moved in spirit and troubled. 'Where have you laid him?' He asked.

"'Come and see, Lord,' they replied.

"Jesus wept."

Why did Jesus cry? (He was sad that Lazarus died and felt bad for everyone who was sad about Lazarus dying.)

Jesus cares about us and feels sad for us when bad things happen to us.

(Read John 11:36-39.)

"Then the Jews said, 'See how He loved him!'

"But some of them said, 'Could not He who opened the eyes of the blind man have kept this man from dying?'

"Jesus, once more deeply moved, came to the tomb. It was a cave with a stone laid across the entrance. 'Take away the stone,' He said.

"'But, Lord,' said Martha, the sister of the dead man, 'by this time there is a bad odor, for he has been there four days.'"

Back then, they buried people by putting them in a cave and rolling a big rock in front of the cave. That's what they did to Lazarus. He died, so they put him in the cave and rolled the rock in front of it. Now, Jesus is telling people to roll the rock out of the way of the cave. Why do you think Jesus wants them to move the rock?

(Read John 11:40-44.)

"Then Jesus said, 'Did I not tell you that if you believe, you will see the glory of God?'

"So they took away the stone. Then Jesus looked up and said, 'Father, I thank You that you have heard Me. I knew that You always hear Me, but I said this for the benefit of the people standing here, that they may believe that You sent Me.'

"When He had said this, Jesus called in a loud voice, 'Lazarus, come out!' The dead man came out, his hands and feet wrapped with strips of linen, and a cloth around his face.

"Jesus said to them, 'Take off the grave clothes and let him go.'

What did Jesus do for Lazarus? (He brought him back to life.)

And Jesus will bring all of us back to life one day too. When Jesus comes back, He will bring everyone who has died back to life, and we will live with Him forever.

How did Jesus raise Lazarus from the dead? (God gave Him the power.)

Jesus prayed and then, He just told Lazarus to come out. When we have a problem, we have to remember to pray and trust that Jesus is powerful enough to help us with it. Jesus is powerful enough to bring dead people back to life. He can do anything.

But do you remember how Mary and Martha sent Jesus the message about Lazarus being sick? Why didn't Jesus go help Lazarus right away and heal him? Why did Jesus wait until Lazarus died to help him?

Jesus knew that the best thing was to wait and raise Lazarus from the dead so that people would believe in Him even more. You have to believe that Jesus knows the best thing for you too. When you have problems, you can trust that even if Jesus doesn't help you right away. He will help you the best way possible. You only have to wait.

(Read John 11:45-53.)

"Therefore many of the Jews who had come to visit Mary, and had seen what Jesus did, believed in Him. But some of them went to the Pharisees and told them what Jesus had done. Then the chief priests and the Pharisees called a meeting of the Sanhedrin.

"'What are we accomplishing?' they asked. 'Here is this man performing many signs. If we let Him go on like this, everyone will believe in Him, and then the Romans will come and take away both our temple and our nation.'

"Then one of them, named Caiaphas, who was high priest that year, spoke up, 'You know nothing at all! You do not realize that it is better for you that one man die for the people than that the whole nation perish.'

"He did not say this on his own, but as high priest that year he prophesied that Jesus would die for the Jewish nation, and not only for that nation but also for the scattered children of God, to bring them together and make them one. So from that day on they plotted to take His life."

Why did the priests want to kill Jesus?

He was getting too powerful. People were listening to Jesus instead of to the priests, and they didn't like that. The priests wanted people to only listen to them.

They were also afraid that the Romans might come and make war on them for letting Jesus get too powerful. The Romans wanted people to serve the Roman Emperor, not Jesus. Everyone was getting jealous of Jesus and how much people liked Him instead of them.

Game: Lazarus Tag – Pick one student to be Death and another student to be Jesus. Death is It. When they tag someone, that person must freeze in place, like they're dead. Jesus, however, can tag the person and unfreeze them, just like Jesus brought Lazarus back from the dead. Death cannot tag Jesus. Play as long as time allows, switching roles every so often so that everyone gets to be Death and Jesus.

Craft: Looking Forward – Remind students that when Jesus comes back, He will bring everyone who believed in Him to back to life to live with Him forever. Then, give them drawing supplies and have them draw them a picture with someone who has died but whom Jesus will bring back to life. It could be a relative or someone famous they'd like to meet.

Closing Prayer: Jesus, we thank You that You will raise all of Your believers back to life one day, just like You raised Lazarus from the dead. Help us to keep believing in You and looking forward to that day. Amen.

Recommended Extras

Superbook: Lazarus – an animated video from the updated Superbook series, includes time-traveling children who learn lessons from the story

Jesus Makes Lazarus Live – free coloring and activity pages

> https://freesundayschoolcurriculum.weebly.com/uploads/1/2/5/0/12503916/lesson_25_jesus_makes_lazarus_live.pdf

Jesus Raises Lazarus – free coloring page

> http://www.sermons4kids.com/raising_lazarus_colorpg.htm

Mary Pours Perfume on Jesus

Use this children's Sunday School lesson to teach kids about giving Jesus our best.

Needed: Bibles, drawing paper, crayons or colored pencils, soft balls or paper wads

Intro Game: What to Do with It? – Divide students into groups of two or three. Tell each group to pretend that you gave them $20. Their job is to come up with the best way to use that money for Jesus. Tell them not to simply say that they would give it to the church. If they do, they have to say what they would want the church to do with that money.

Each group then presents their answer to the class. After each group has given their answer, have the whole class vote on the best idea. Students cannot vote for their own group's answer.

Do the same thing for $1,000 and then, for $1 million.

Lesson: Read John 12:1-3.

"Six days before the Passover, Jesus came to Bethany, where Lazarus lived, whom Jesus had raised from the dead. Here a dinner was given in Jesus' honor. Martha served, while Lazarus was among those reclining at the table with Him. Then Mary took about a pint of pure nard, an expensive perfume; she poured it on Jesus' feet and wiped His feet with her hair. And the house was filled with the fragrance of the perfume."

Why did Mary use such an expensive perfume on Jesus and wipe His feet with her hair? (She is worshipping Jesus. Jesus deserves the best that we can give Him.)

What are some things that you can do to worship Jesus and give Him your best? (Ideas could include being good because Jesus wants us to be good, giving Jesus our offerings, using our talents for God, giving God the glory for our talents, spending time with Him by reading our Bibles, praying, going to church, etc.)

(Read John 12:4-6.)

"But one of His disciples, Judas Iscariot, who was later to betray Him, objected, 'Why wasn't this perfume sold and the money given to the poor? It was worth a year's wages.' He did not say this because he cared about the poor but because he was a thief; as keeper of the money bag, he used to help himself to what was put into it."

Why did Judas not want Mary to use the perfume on Jesus? (He was greedy and thought that he could have sold the perfume and gotten a lot of money for it. He was more worried about what he could get than about worshipping Jesus.)

(Read John 12:7-11.)

"'Leave her alone,' Jesus replied. 'It was intended that she should save this perfume for the day of My burial. You will always have the poor among you, but you will not always have Me.'

"Meanwhile a large crowd of Jews found out that Jesus was there and came, not only because of Him but also to see Lazarus, whom He had raised from the dead. So the chief priests made plans to kill Lazarus as well, for on account of him many of the Jews were going over to Jesus and believing in Him."

Why did the priests want to kill Jesus?

Jesus was getting too powerful, and the priests were getting jealous of Him. People were listening to Jesus instead of to the priests, especially after Jesus raised Lazarus from the dead, and the priests didn't like that. The priests wanted people to only listen to them.

Did Jesus know He was going to die? (Yes. He told the disciples that Mary had put the perfume on Him to get His body ready to be buried.)

Jesus knew He was going to die because that's what He came to do. He came to die on the cross to take the punishment for our sin so that we could be forgiven.

Craft: Giving Jesus Our Best – Give students drawing supplies and have them draw a picture of themselves doing something to give Jesus their best. When they're finished, have them tell the class about their picture.

Game: Taking Our Place – Play a game of dodgeball with soft play balls or paper wads. When one team starts to accumulate a lot of players in the "Out" zone, run in and say that you'll take their place being out. They can get back in the game. Do the same for the other team. Keep doing it as long as time allows. Then, explain that just like you were taking the place of people who were out, Jesus took our place on the cross. He took our punishment so that we could be forgiven for our sins.

An alternative is a game of two-team tag. Take the place of students who are tagged and out of the game.

Closing Prayer: Jesus, we thank You for coming to take our punishment so that we could be forgiven for our sins. Help us to always give You our best because of what You did for us. Amen.

Recommended Extra

Mary Pours Perfume on Jesus' Feet – free coloring page

http://sermons4kids.com/jesus-forgives-colorpg.htm

Palm Sunday – Jesus Rides into Jerusalem on a Donkey

Use this children's Sunday School lesson to teach kids about both Jesus' identity and the need to respect the church as a holy place.

Needed: Bibles, construction paper, old clothes, balloons

Worship Activity: Mini Church Service – To help kids understand that the church is a holy place, take some time to walk through the elements of a church service. Do any or all of the following:

Sing a praise song.
Choose a student to lead a prayer.
Choose a student to tell what a Bible passage or verse means.
Choose one or more students to give a testimony or praise.
Take an offering.
Choose a student to make an announcement.

After each element, ask how that action helps us give respect to God.

Lesson: Read Matthew 21:1-3.

"As they approached Jerusalem and came to Bethphage on the Mount of Olives, Jesus sent two disciples, saying to them, 'Go to the village ahead of you, and at once you will find a donkey tied there, with her colt by her. Untie them and bring them to Me. If anyone says anything to you, say that the Lord needs them, and he will send them right away.'"

How did Jesus know that there would be a donkey in a certain spot for Him to ride on? (God knows everything and God told Jesus about where the donkey would be.)

(Read Matthew 21:4-11.)

"This took place to fulfill what was spoken through the prophet: 'Say to Daughter Zion, "See, your king comes to you, gentle and riding on a donkey, and on a colt, the foal of a donkey."'

"The disciples went and did as Jesus had instructed them. They brought the donkey and the colt and placed their cloaks on them for Jesus to sit on. A very large crowd spread their cloaks on the road, while others cut branches from the trees and spread them on the road. The crowds that went ahead of Him and those that followed shouted,

"'Hosanna to the Son of David!

"'Blessed is He who comes in the name of the Lord!'

"'Hosanna in the highest heaven!'

When Jesus entered Jerusalem, the whole city was stirred and asked, 'Who is this?'

"The crowds answered, 'This is Jesus, the prophet from Nazareth in Galilee.'

Why were all the people waving palm branches for Jesus and putting their clothes on the road for His donkey to walk on?

They had seen and heard about all the miracles He had been doing. They believed that Jesus was a great prophet from God and were waving the branches to welcome Him into Jerusalem. They believed that Jesus should be their new king. It's like they were having a parade for Him.

(Read Matthew 21:12-13.)

"Jesus entered the temple courts and drove out all who were buying and selling there. He overturned the tables of the money changers and the benches of those selling doves. 'It is written,' He said to them, '"My house will be called a house of prayer," but you are making it "a den of robbers."'

Why did Jesus wreck the stuff of the people selling things in the Temple?

The Temple was the church for the people back then. The church is supposed to be a special place where people can come and pray and worship God. It isn't supposed to be used for a store or for a place where people try to make money.

(Read Matthew 21:14-15.)

"The blind and the lame came to Him at the temple, and He healed them. But when the chief priests and the teachers of the law saw the wonderful things He did and the children shouting in the temple courts, 'Hosanna to the Son of David,' they were indignant."

What were the children saying about Jesus? (Hosanna to the Son of David!)

It means, "Praise to the Son of David." They were saying it to Jesus because they knew Jesus was a descendant of King David. The children knew who Jesus was, and Jesus loves it when children praise Him!

Game: Palm Tree Parade Relay – Cut out palm leaves from construction paper and gather clothes into two piles. Divide kids into two teams. Place the piles of clothes at the end of the room.

Teams must relay to lay out the clothes from their team's starting line to the clothes pile, so the first student from each teams runs down to the clothes pile, then brings something back to lay right in front of their team's line. The second student runs down and lays a second piece of clothing in front of the first until the teams have a line of clothes stretching from the team's line to the original pile of clothes.

Each student then must take turns getting a balloon down and back by waving their palm leaves to push it along their clothes path.

Remind students about how the people waved palm branches and laid their clothes on the road when Jesus came into Jerusalem.

Closing Prayer: Jesus, You are the King. Help us to worship You like You deserve and respect Your church as a holy place. Amen.

Recommended Extra

The King is Coming! – free object lesson, along with free coloring and activity pages

https://www.sermons4kids.com/king-is-coming.html

Recommended Extras for the Last Supper

Superbook: The Last Supper – an animated video from the updated Superbook series, includes time-traveling children who learn lessons from the story

God's Story: The Last Supper – free 3-4-minute video explaining Jesus washing His disciples' feet and the first Communion

>https://ministry-to-children.com/video-last-supper-story-for-kids/

Jesus Washes His Disciples' Feet and The Last Supper– free coloring and activity pages

>https://freesundayschoolcurriculum.weebly.com/uploads/1/2/5/0/12503916/lesson_26_jesus_washes_his_disciples_feet.pdf

>https://freesundayschoolcurriculum.weebly.com/uploads/1/2/5/0/12503916/lesson_66_the_last_supper.pdf

Jesus Teaches His Disciples How to Serve One Another

Use this children's Sunday School lesson to teach children about serving others.

Needed: Bibles, drawing paper, crayons or colored pencils

Intro Game: Good and Faithful Servant – Tell the students that you're going to play a game in which you're the Master, and they're your servants. You're going to name something you want, and they have 15 seconds to bring you what you asked for.

Anything that meets your criteria counts. If a student can't bring you what you asked for within 15 seconds, they're out. Items you already have in front of you count if they can apply it to meet the new criteria. The last one in the game wins and becomes the Master for the next round.

Some ideas of what to ask for include:

Something of a certain color
Something of a certain shape
Something that reminds you of the Bible
Something that reminds you of Jesus
Something you would use for a certain purpose

Part of the fun could be naming criteria that a lot of items meet and then narrowing it down to criteria that only a few items in your area meet.

Play 2-3 rounds and then explain that they were all good servants because they all tried to bring you what you asked for. Even though some of them couldn't find what you wanted, none of them said they wouldn't do it. They all tried.

Lesson: Ask students, Who do you think is the greatest person who ever lived?

Who do you think is greater, people who have servants, or the servants? People who are bosses, or people who listen to the boss? The king or the people in the kingdom? The President or the rest of the people in the country?

If you're the greatest person in the world, do you think you would have people working for you, or would you work for other people?

(Read John 13:1.)

"It was just before the Passover Festival. Jesus knew that the hour had come for Him to leave this world and go to the Father. Having loved His own who were in the world, He loved them to the end."

Did Jesus know He was going to die soon? (Yes.)

The reason Jesus came to Earth was to die on the cross to take our punishment so that we could be forgiven for our sins.

(Read John 13:2-8.)

"The evening meal was in progress, and the devil had already prompted Judas, the son of Simon Iscariot, to betray Jesus. Jesus knew that the Father had put all things under His power, and that He had come from God and was returning to God; so He got up from the meal, took off His outer clothing, and wrapped a towel around His waist. After that, He poured water into a basin and began to wash His disciples' feet, drying them with the towel that was wrapped around Him.

"He came to Simon Peter, who said to him, 'Lord, are you going to wash my feet?'

"Jesus replied, 'You do not realize now what I am doing, but later you will understand.'

"'No,' said Peter, 'You shall never wash my feet.'

"Jesus answered, 'Unless I wash you, you have no part with Me.'"

Why didn't Peter want Jesus to wash his feet?

Peter knew that Jesus is God and that Jesus is the greatest person who ever lived. People should be doing things for Jesus instead of Jesus doing things for other people.

(Read John 13:9-15.)

"'Then, Lord,' Simon Peter replied, 'not just my feet but my hands and my head as well!'

"Jesus answered, 'Those who have had a bath need only to wash their feet; their whole body is clean. And you are clean, though not every one of you.' For He knew who was going to betray Him, and that was why He said not every one was clean.

"When He had finished washing their feet, He put on His clothes and returned to His place. 'Do you understand what I have done for you?' He asked them. 'You call me 'Teacher' and 'Lord,' and rightly so, for that is what I am. Now that I, your Lord and Teacher, have washed your feet, you also should wash one another's feet. I have set you an example that you should do as I have done for you.'"

Why did Jesus wash His disciples' feet? (To give them an example of what they are supposed to do)

Everyone is supposed to do things for other people. No one is just supposed to have people do things for them. Everyone is equal, and everyone is supposed to do things for others instead of thinking that they're greater than someone else. No one is greater than anyone else. Only Jesus is greater because He was part of God. Other people are just regular people. We're all the same.

(Read John 13:16.)

"Very truly I tell you, no servant is greater than his master, nor is a messenger greater than the one who sent him."

Jesus was the Master, and the disciples were the servants. The disciples were the messenger, and Jesus was the one who sent them.

Jesus says that if even He did things for other people, then the disciples have to do things for other people too. They're not more important than Jesus, so they can't say that they don't have to do something that Jesus did.

(Read John 13:17.)

"Now that you know these things, you will be blessed if you do them."

If we know that Jesus told us to do things for other people, and we do them, what will happen to us? (We will be blessed.)

God will reward us if we listen to Jesus and do things for other people as He said.

Craft: Serving Suggestion – Give students drawing supplies and have them draw a picture of themselves doing something for someone else. When they're finished, have them tell the class about their picture.

Game: Good and Faithful Servant – Play the intro game again and emphasize they're serving the Master by getting what they want but that then, they get a chance to be served by others. We're all supposed to serve each other.

Closing Prayer: Jesus, we thank You for setting the example of how we should treat other people. Help us to think of ways that we can serve others as You did. Amen.

Last Supper - Communion

Use this children's Sunday School lesson to teach children about what the sacrament means and how Jesus started it at the Last Supper.

Needed: Bibles, a Communion set (It's up to you whether your church will allow you to have Communion with the children. If not, simply show them the items used in Communion.)

Intro Game: Traitor Among Us! – Have students close their eyes. Explain that when you walk among them and tap one student on the shoulder, that student is the Traitor. When you tap them, they should look up and point to another student.

Have everyone open their eyes and say that the student the Traitor pointed to is not the Traitor. Students then have the opportunity to guess who the Traitor is. If they guess more than one person, have them take a vote. If the majority votes for the actual Traitor, they win and the game is over. Choose a new Traitor and play again.

If the majority is wrong, the person the Traitor pointed at is out. Have everyone close their eyes and then, ask the Traitor to point to another student. The game continues until students guess the real Traitor or the Traitor is one of the last two students left. If the Traitor makes it to the end, they win.

Play as long as time allows. Then, explain that one of Jesus' disciples was a traitor.

Lesson: Ask students, What is Communion?

Why do we take Communion?

(Read Matthew 26:14-16.)

"Then one of the Twelve—the one called Judas Iscariot—went to the chief priests and asked, 'What are you willing to give me if I deliver Him over to you?' So they counted out for him thirty pieces of silver. From then on Judas watched for an opportunity to hand Him over."

It says that Judas offered to be a traitor to Jesus and help the priests arrest Jesus. Why would Judas be a traitor to Jesus? (Judas didn't really believe in Jesus. He just wanted to get money from the priests.)

(Read Matthew 26:17-25.)

"On the first day of the Festival of Unleavened Bread, the disciples came to Jesus and asked, 'Where do you want us to make preparations for You to eat the Passover?'

"He replied, 'Go into the city to a certain man and tell him, "The Teacher says: 'My appointed time is near. I am going to celebrate the Passover with my disciples at your house.'"' So the disciples did as Jesus had directed them and prepared the Passover.

"When evening came, Jesus was reclining at the table with the Twelve. And while they were eating, He said, 'Truly I tell you, one of you will betray Me.'

They were very sad and began to say to Him one after the other, 'Surely You don't mean me, Lord?'

"Jesus replied, 'The one who has dipped his hand into the bowl with Me will betray Me. The Son of Man will go just as it is written about Him. But woe to that man who betrays the Son of Man! It would be better for him if he had not been born.'

"Then Judas, the one who would betray Him, said, 'Surely you don't mean me, Rabbi?'

"Jesus answered, 'You have said so.'"

How did Jesus know that Judas was a traitor? (God told Him. God knows everything, even before it happens.)

(Read Matthew 26:26.)

"While they were eating, Jesus took bread, and when He had given thanks, He broke it and gave it to His disciples, saying, 'Take and eat; this is My body.'"

Jesus and His disciples were having the first Communion. What does Jesus say the bread is in Communion? (Jesus' body.)

(Read Matthew 26:27-28.)

"Then He took a cup, and when He had given thanks, He gave it to them, saying, 'Drink from it, all of you. This is My blood of the covenant, which is poured out for many for the forgiveness of sins.'"

What does Jesus say the wine, or grape juice, is in Communion? (Jesus' blood.)

So, when you see the bread being broken for Communion, it's supposed to remind you of all the pain that Jesus went through in His body when He died. And when you see the wine or grape juice being poured into the cup for Communion, it's supposed to remind you of how Jesus bled and died on the cross.

Optional Activity: Administer Communion to your students if this is allowed in your church.

Optional Game: The Life of Jesus Relay – Divide students into two or more teams. When you say, "Go!" the first student on each team will perform the first leg of the relay race, traveling to the other side of your play area and back to their team. The second student on each team then does the second leg, and so on until that team completes the last leg. The first team to complete all legs of the race wins.

Leg 1. Crying. Cry like a baby to show Jesus was born as a baby.

Leg 2. Crawl. Crawl like a baby to show that Jesus had to crawl when he was little.

Leg 3. Slow Walk. Walk slowly like a one-year-old to show that Jesus had to learn to walk.

Leg 4. Run. Run like a child, as Jesus did when He was a boy.

Leg 5. Hammer the Ground. Hit the ground like you're a man hammering nails to show that Jesus learned how to be a carpenter.

Leg 6. Spin. Spin around saying, "You're healed! You're healed!" to show that Jesus helped all the people around Him.

Leg 7. Crucifix Run. Run with your arms outstretched to the sides to show that Jesus was crucified on a cross.

Leg 8. Backward Walk. Walk backward with your arms crossed over your chest to show that Jesus died.

Leg 9. Skip. Skip, yelling, "Ta-da!" to show that Jesus came back to life.

Game: Traitor Among Us! – Play the intro game and remind students that Judas betrayed Jesus.

Closing Prayer: Jesus, we thank You for coming to die on the cross to take the punishment for our sin. Help us to believe in

You just like Your disciples did during that first Communion. Amen.

Good Friday and Easter Recommended Extras

Washed Clean — a free demonstration that uses food coloring and bleach to show how Jesus' death and resurrection takes away our sins

> https://ministry-to-children.com/washed-clean-easter-object-lesson/

Jesus Prays in the Garden, Two Disciples Fail Jesus, Jesus Dies on the Cross, and Jesus is Buried — free coloring and activity pages

> https://freesundayschoolcurriculum.weebly.com/uploads/1/2/5/0/12503916/lesson_69_jesus_prays_in_the_garden.pdf
>
> https://freesundayschoolcurriculum.weebly.com/uploads/1/2/5/0/12503916/lesson_70_two_disciples_fail_jesus.pdf
>
> https://freesundayschoolcurriculum.weebly.com/uploads/1/2/5/0/12503916/lesson_71_jesus_dies_on_the_cross.pdf
>
> https://freesundayschoolcurriculum.weebly.com/uploads/1/2/5/0/12503916/lesson_72_jesus_is_buried.pdf

From Cheers to Jeers — free object lesson, along with free coloring and activity pages

> https://www.sermons4kids.com/cheers2jeers.html

Superbook: He is Risen! — an animated video from the updated Superbook series, includes time-traveling children who learn lessons from the story

Greatest Adventures Stories from the Bible: The Easter Story – animated video with time-traveling teenagers who witness the Biblical story, realistic art style

Greatest Heroes and Legends of the Bible: Last Supper, Crucifixion, and Resurrection – another animated video with a Disneyesque art style and no time traveling

God's Story: Easter – a free video telling the story of Jesus, along with application, in about four and a half minutes

> https://ministry-to-children.com/easter-gods-story-video-clip-for-kids/

Family Life Resurrection Eggs – a set of Easter Eggs with different items inside representing elements of the Easter story

Easter Stickers – an alternative to Easter candy that also reminds kids of the reason for the holy day

He is Alive Easter Lesson – a free lesson that includes a neat activity in which the author recommends placing various items related to the story of Jesus' death and resurrection in plastic Easter eggs. Kids search for the eggs, open them, and talk about what they know of the Easter story.

> https://ministry-to-children.com/he-is-alive-easter-lesson/

God Colors Our Lives – a free object lesson that uses colored Easter eggs to demonstrate how God makes our lives vibrant and exciting

> https://ministry-to-children.com/object-lessons-easter-egg/

Jesus Rises from the Dead – free coloring and activity pages

> https://freesundayschoolcurriculum.weebly.com/uploads/1/2/5/0/12503916/lesson_73_jesus_rises_from_the_dead.pdf

The Stone was Rolled Away! – free object lesson, along with free coloring and activity pages

> https://www.sermons4kids.com/rolled-away.html

Jesus is Arrested

Use this children's Sunday School lesson to teach kids about Jesus praying in the Garden, Judas' betrayal, and Peter's denial.

Needed: Bibles, dice

Intro Game: Traitor Among Us! – Have students close their eyes. Explain that when you walk among them and tap one student on the shoulder, that student is the Traitor. When you tap them, they should look up and point to another student.

Have everyone open their eyes and say that the student the Traitor pointed to is not the Traitor. Students then have the opportunity to guess who the Traitor is. If they guess more than one person, have them take a vote. If the majority votes for the actual Traitor, they win and the game is over. Choose a new Traitor and play again.

If the majority is wrong, the person the Traitor pointed at is out. Have everyone close their eyes and then, ask the Traitor to point to another student. The game continues until students guess the real Traitor or the Traitor is one of the last two students left. If the Traitor makes it to the end, they win.

Play as long as time allows. Then, explain that one of Jesus' disciples was a traitor.

Alternative Intro Game: Jesus Betrayed! – Choose one student to be Jesus. Then, have "Jesus" turn around and choose one of the other students to be the Traitor.

"Jesus" then tries to tag all the other students, but if they tag the Traitor, they're out. "Jesus" wins when they tag everyone except the Traitor.

Explain that Jesus chose His disciples, but one of them was a traitor.

Lesson: Tell students, The Bible story we're about to read takes place right after Jesus washed His disciples' feet and gave them Communion for the first time.

(Read Matthew 26:30-34.)

"When they had sung a hymn, they went out to the Mount of Olives. Then Jesus told them, 'This very night you will all fall away on account of Me, for it is written: "I will strike the shepherd, and the sheep of the flock will be scattered."

"'But after I have risen, I will go ahead of you into Galilee.'

"Peter replied, 'Even if all fall away on account of You, I never will.'

"'Truly I tell you,' Jesus answered, 'this very night, before the rooster crows, you will disown Me three times.'"

How did Jesus know that Peter would deny knowing Him? (God told Him. God knows everything even before it happens.)

(Read Matthew 26:36-38.)

"Then Jesus went with His disciples to a place called Gethsemane, and He said to them, 'Sit here while I go over there and pray.' He took Peter and the two sons of Zebedee along with Him, and He began to be sorrowful and troubled. Then He said to them, 'My soul is overwhelmed with sorrow to the point of death. Stay here and keep watch with Me.'"

Jesus said that He was sad. Why do you think He would be sad? (Jesus knew that He was going to die on the cross soon and was afraid because He knew it would hurt.)

Why did Jesus want His friends to pray with Him?

It's good to help support each other in prayer.

What do you think Jesus wanted the disciples to pray about?

He might have wanted them to pray that He would brave and do what God wanted Him to do. Maybe He wanted to pray for themselves for God to help them stay strong and keep believing in Him when He was arrested and put to death on the cross.

(Read Matthew 26:39-44.)

"Going a little farther, He fell with His face to the ground and prayed, 'My Father, if it is possible, may this cup be taken from Me. Yet not as I will, but as You will.'

"Then He returned to His disciples and found them sleeping. 'Couldn't you men keep watch with me for one hour?' He asked Peter. 'Watch and pray so that you will not fall into temptation. The spirit is willing, but the flesh is weak.'

"He went away a second time and prayed, 'My Father, if it is not possible for this cup to be taken away unless I drink it, may Your will be done.'

"When He came back, He again found them sleeping, because their eyes were heavy. So He left them and went away once more and prayed the third time, saying the same thing."

What did Jesus decide about His dying?

He decided to do what God wanted Him to do and die. He wanted God to make it so that He wouldn't have to die, but He said He would die if it was God's will.

Even though it was hard, Jesus was willing to die because He knew that's what God wanted Him to do so that He could save us. Jesus loved us and wanted to save us so much that He was willing to die on the cross.

Sometimes, God might ask us to do something hard, too, and we have to be willing to do it because God always has a good reason for telling us to do something. If we listen to God, everything will always work out for the best.

(Read Matthew 26:45-54.)

"Then He returned to the disciples and said to them, 'Are you still sleeping and resting? Look, the hour has come, and the Son of Man is delivered into the hands of sinners. Rise! Let us go! Here comes my betrayer!'

"While he was still speaking, Judas, one of the Twelve, arrived. With him was a large crowd armed with swords and clubs, sent from the chief priests and the elders of the people. Now the betrayer had arranged a signal with them: 'The one I kiss is the man; arrest him.' Going at once to Jesus, Judas said, 'Greetings, Rabbi!' and kissed Him.

"Jesus replied, 'Do what you came for, friend.'

"Then the men stepped forward, seized Jesus and arrested Him. With that, one of Jesus' companions reached for his sword, drew it out and struck the servant of the high priest, cutting off his ear.

"'Put your sword back in its place,' Jesus said to him, 'for all who draw the sword will die by the sword. Do you think I cannot call on My Father, and He will at once put at My disposal more than twelve legions of angels? But how then would the Scriptures be fulfilled that say it must happen in this way?'"

Peter attacked one of the guards that came to arrest Jesus, but Jesus told Peter to put his sword away. Why do you think Jesus didn't want Peter to fight the guards? (Jesus knew that He had to be arrested so that He could die as the punishment for our sins.)

(Read Matthew 26:55-64.)

"In that hour Jesus said to the crowd, 'Am I leading a rebellion, that you have come out with swords and clubs to capture Me? Every day I sat in the temple courts teaching, and you did not arrest Me. But this has all taken place that the writings of the prophets might be fulfilled.' Then all the disciples deserted Him and fled.

"Those who had arrested Jesus took Him to Caiaphas the high priest, where the teachers of the law and the elders had assembled. But Peter followed Him at a distance, right up to the courtyard of the high priest. He entered and sat down with the guards to see the outcome.

"The chief priests and the whole Sanhedrin were looking for false evidence against Jesus so that they could put Him to death. But they did not find any, though many false witnesses came forward.

"Finally two came forward and declared, 'This fellow said, "I am able to destroy the temple of God and rebuild it in three days."'

"Then the high priest stood up and said to Jesus, 'Are You not going to answer? What is this testimony that these men are bringing against You?' But Jesus remained silent.

"The high priest said to Him, 'I charge you under oath by the living God: Tell us if you are the Messiah, the Son of God.'

"'You have said so,' Jesus replied. 'But I say to all of you: From now on you will see the Son of Man sitting at the right hand of the Mighty One and coming on the clouds of heaven.'"

Jesus said that in the future, everyone would see Him coming with power out of the clouds. What do you think that means?

Jesus will come back out of the sky one day and will judge everyone in the whole world, sending those people who don't believe in Him to Hell and bringing everyone who does believe in Him back to life and making them live forever.

(Read Matthew 26:65-72.)

"Then the high priest tore his clothes and said, 'He has spoken blasphemy! Why do we need any more witnesses? Look, now you have heard the blasphemy. What do you think?'

"'He is worthy of death,' they answered.

"Then they spit in His face and struck Him with their fists. Others slapped him and said, 'Prophesy to us, Messiah. Who hit you?'

"Now Peter was sitting out in the courtyard, and a servant girl came to him. 'You also were with Jesus of Galilee,' she said.

"But he denied it before them all. 'I don't know what you're talking about,' he said.

"Then he went out to the gateway, where another servant girl saw him and said to the people there, 'This fellow was with Jesus of Nazareth.'

"He denied it again, with an oath: 'I don't know the man!'"

Why did Peter say that he didn't know Jesus? (He was afraid and thought that he might be arrested, too, for being Jesus' follower.)

But we should never be afraid to tell people that we're followers of Jesus. We should never be embarrassed to say we believe in Jesus.

(Read Matthew 26:73-75.)

"After a little while, those standing there went up to Peter and said, 'Surely you are one of them; your accent gives you away.'

"Then he began to call down curses, and he swore to them, 'I don't know the man!'

"Immediately a rooster crowed. Then Peter remembered the word Jesus had spoken: 'Before the rooster crows, you will disown Me three times.' And he went outside and wept bitterly."

Why was Peter crying? (He felt bad for saying he didn't know Jesus.)

(Read Matthew 27:1-5.)

"Early in the morning, all the chief priests and the elders of the people made their plans how to have Jesus executed. So they bound Him, led Him away and handed Him over to Pilate the governor.

"When Judas, who had betrayed Him, saw that Jesus was condemned, he was seized with remorse and returned the thirty pieces of silver to the chief priests and the elders. 'I have sinned,' he said, 'for I have betrayed innocent blood.'

"'What is that to us?' they replied. 'That's your responsibility.'

"So Judas threw the money into the temple and left. Then he went away and hanged himself."

Why did Judas give back the money and then hang himself? (He felt guilty for being a traitor to Jesus and telling the guards where to find Him so that they could arrest Him.)

Was it good for Judas to hang himself? (No.)

What should he have done instead? (He should have asked God to forgive him.)

When we do something wrong, we should ask God for forgiveness. God will always forgive us when we ask Him to because He loves us.

Game: Raising the Dice – Remind students that Jesus wanted His disciples to pray with Him before He was arrested. Then, divide students into two teams and give each time a six-sided die. The first student from each team runs up to a table and rolls their dice. The student with the highest roll gets a point for their team.

The trick is that each team can help their player. As the students are rolling their die, the teams cheer. The team that's the loudest gets to add one number to their player's die roll. So, if Team A's player rolls a 3, but their team is cheering the loudest, you'll count that player's roll as a 4.

Students re-roll in case of a tie, but only if the tie occurs after you add the cheering bonus.

After the first two students roll and you determine who gets the point, those students run back to their teams, hand off their die, and the next students run up. The team with the most points after everyone has rolled wins.

Explain that when we pray for someone, it's like we're cheering for them. We're asking God to help them.

Game: Traitor Among Us! or **Jesus Betrayed!** – Play one of the intro games again and remind students that even though Judas betrayed Jesus, he could have asked God to forgive him, and God would have. God will always forgive us if we ask Him to.

Closing Prayer: Jesus, we thank You for being willing to die on the cross to take our punishment. And we thank You that You always forgive us. Help us to trust in You as we wait for You to come back and make it so that we can live forever with You. Amen.

Jesus Dies and Takes Away Our Sins

Use this children's Sunday School lesson to teach children about how Jesus died for us to forgive us for our sins.

Needed: Bibles, rotten food, candy bars, newspaper or other paper, Silly Putty or the following: food coloring, white glue, liquid starch (like Sta-Flo for laundry), measuring cups, sandwich baggies

Intro Game: Taking Our Place – Divide students into two teams for a game of Freeze Tag. Choose one team to be It, chasing the other team. Then, choose one student from the team being chased. They are "Jesus." They cannot be tagged. They can go stand in the place of a frozen team member, allowing them to run again. When "Jesus" takes the place of someone else, they must stay there for 3 seconds since Jesus was in the grave for three days.

Before the game, set a timer for 3 or 5 minutes, depending on how many students you have. If the team chasing the other gets everyone out within that time limit, they win. If they don't, the team being chased wins.

Switch roles and play again.

Lesson: Read Matthew 27:11.

"Meanwhile Jesus stood before the governor, and the governor asked Him, 'Are you the king of the Jews?'

"'You have said so,' Jesus replied."

Why did Pilate ask Jesus if He was the King of the Jews?

If Jesus was a king, He might have tried to take over the country and fight the Romans ,and Pilate can't let Jesus start a war against the Romans because Pilate works for the Roman government.

Why did Jesus say that He is the King of the Jews?

Jesus is the descendant of King David, which means He is the rightful King. Jesus is also God, so He is the King of everything.

(Read Matthew 27:12-14.)

"When He was accused by the chief priests and the elders, He gave no answer. Then Pilate asked Him, 'Don't you hear the testimony they are bringing against You?' But Jesus made no reply, not even to a single charge—to the great amazement of the governor."

Why didn't Jesus answer any more of Pilate's questions?

Jesus didn't want to defend Himself. He knew He was supposed to let Pilate crucify Him so that He could die for our sins.

(Read Matthew 27:15-46.)

"Now it was the governor's custom at the festival to release a prisoner chosen by the crowd. At that time they had a well-known prisoner whose name was Jesus Barabbas. So when the crowd had gathered, Pilate asked them, 'Which one do you want me to release to you: Jesus Barabbas, or Jesus who is called the Messiah?' For he knew it was out of self-interest that they had handed Jesus over to him.

"While Pilate was sitting on the judge's seat, his wife sent him this message: 'Don't have anything to do with that innocent man, for I have suffered a great deal today in a dream because of Him.'

"But the chief priests and the elders persuaded the crowd to ask for Barabbas and to have Jesus executed.

"'Which of the two do you want me to release to you?' asked the governor.

"'Barabbas,' they answered.

"'What shall I do, then, with Jesus who is called the Messiah?' Pilate asked.

"They all answered, 'Crucify Him!'

"'Why? What crime has he committed?' asked Pilate.

"But they shouted all the louder, 'Crucify Him!'

"When Pilate saw that he was getting nowhere, but that instead an uproar was starting, he took water and washed his hands in front of the crowd. 'I am innocent of this man's blood,' he said. 'It is your responsibility!'

"All the people answered, 'His blood is on us and on our children!'

"Then he released Barabbas to them. But he had Jesus flogged, and handed Him over to be crucified.

"Then the governor's soldiers took Jesus into the Praetorium and gathered the whole company of soldiers around Him. They stripped Him and put a scarlet robe on Him, and then twisted together a crown of thorns and set it on His head. They put a staff in His right hand. Then they knelt in front of Him and mocked Him. 'Hail, king of the Jews!' they said. They spit on Him, and took the staff and struck Him on the head again and again. After they had mocked Him, they took off the robe and put His own clothes on Him. Then they led Him away to crucify Him.

"As they were going out, they met a man from Cyrene, named Simon, and they forced him to carry the cross. They came to a place called Golgotha (which means 'the place of the skull'). There they offered Jesus wine to drink, mixed with gall; but after tasting it, He refused to drink it. When they had crucified Him, they divided up His clothes by casting lots. And sitting down, they kept watch over Him there. Above His head they placed the written charge against Him: this is Jesus, the king of the Jews.

"Two rebels were crucified with Him, one on His right and one on His left. Those who passed by hurled insults at Him, shaking their heads and saying, 'You who are going to destroy the temple and build it in three days, save Yourself! Come down from the cross, if you are the Son of God!' In the same way the chief priests, the teachers of the law and the elders mocked Him. 'He saved others,' they said, 'but He can't save Himself! He's the king of Israel! Let Him come down now from the cross, and we will believe in Him. He trusts in God. Let God rescue Him now if He wants Him, for He said, 'I am the Son of God.'' In the same way the rebels who were crucified with Him also heaped insults on Him.

"From noon until three in the afternoon darkness came over all the land. About three in the afternoon Jesus cried out in a loud voice, 'Eli, Eli, lema sabachthani?' (which means 'My God, my God, why have You forsaken Me?')."

When Jesus was on the cross, why did He say, "My God, My God, why have You forsaken Me?"

Jesus had taken all the sins of everyone in the whole world on Himself. He had to take our sins on Himself so that He could take away our sins for us and save us.

But having all those sins on Him meant that God didn't want to be with Him. When we have sin in our lives, God doesn't want to be with us because God doesn't want to be around people who do bad things. If we ask for forgiveness and stop doing bad things, then God will come to be with us again.

(Read Matthew 27:47-61.)

"When some of those standing there heard this, they said, 'He's calling Elijah.'

"Immediately one of them ran and got a sponge. He filled it with wine vinegar, put it on a staff, and offered it to Jesus to drink. The rest said, 'Now leave Him alone. Let's see if Elijah comes to save Him.'

"And when Jesus had cried out again in a loud voice, He gave up His spirit.

"At that moment the curtain of the temple was torn in two from top to bottom. The earth shook, the rocks split and the tombs broke open. The bodies of many holy people who had died were raised to life. They came out of the tombs after Jesus' resurrection and went into the holy city and appeared to many people.

When the centurion and those with him who were guarding Jesus saw the earthquake and all that had happened, they were terrified, and exclaimed, 'Surely He was the Son of God!'

"Many women were there, watching from a distance. They had followed Jesus from Galilee to care for His needs. Among them were Mary Magdalene, Mary the mother of James and Joseph, and the mother of Zebedee's sons.

"As evening approached, there came a rich man from Arimathea, named Joseph, who had himself become a disciple of Jesus. Going to Pilate, he asked for Jesus' body, and Pilate ordered that it be given to him. Joseph took the body, wrapped it in a clean linen cloth, and placed it in his own new tomb that he had cut out of the rock. He rolled a big stone in front of the entrance to the tomb and went away. Mary Magdalene and the other Mary were sitting there opposite the tomb."

Object Lesson: Give kids something unpleasant, such as a rotten banana or something. Have a row of good prizes lined up, like candy bars. Ask each child if they'd like to keep what they have (the bad thing) or trade it for one of the prizes. It should be a no-brainer.

After everyone has made their choice, explain that Jesus takes our sin and gives us the best thing of all, life forever with God.

Craft: Taking Our Sin – Have students make silly putty or bring some in for each student. Have them practice using the silly putty to copy print or pictures off of a newspaper or other printed paper.

After they've played with it for a few minutes, explain that Jesus took our sins on Himself when He died on the cross.

To make silly putty: Tell students to pour 1/4 cup of white glue, a few drops of food coloring, and 1/8 cup of liquid starch into a sandwich baggie. Close the baggie and knead the mixture with your fingers through the baggie until it gains the right consistency. If it is not hardening properly, add a little more liquid starch.

Game: Taking Our Place – Play the intro game again, reminding students that Jesus took our place when He took our punishment and died on the cross for us.

Closing Prayer: Jesus, we thank You for taking the punishment for our sins so that we could be forgiven. Help us to believe and trust in You always. Amen.

The Real Meaning of the Easter Basket

Use this children's Sunday School lesson to teach kids the symbolism of the Easter basket.

Needed: Easter basket, Easter grass, chocolate coins or chocolate with some kind of shiny wrapping (Hershey's Kisses, York Peppermint Patties, etc.), chicken or rooster-shaped candy (a chocolate rooster, or chick-shaped Peeps), a plastic egg with something inside of it, rolls of toilet paper, cones or another place marker

Intro Game: The Life of Jesus Relay – Divide students into two or more teams. When you say, "Go!" the first student on each team will perform the first leg of the relay race, traveling to the other side of your play area and back to their team. The second student on each team then does the second leg, and so on until that team completes the last leg. The first team to complete all legs of the race wins.

Leg 1. Crying. Cry like a baby to show Jesus was born as a baby.

Leg 2. Crawl. Crawl like a baby to show that Jesus had to crawl when he was little.

Leg 3. Slow Walk. Walk slowly like a one-year-old to show that Jesus had to learn to walk.

Leg 4. Run. Run like a child, as Jesus did when He was a boy.

Leg 5. Hammer the Ground. Hit the ground like you're a man hammering nails to show that Jesus learned how to be a carpenter.

Leg 6. Spin. Spin around saying, "You're healed! You're healed!" to show that Jesus helped all the people around Him.

Leg 7. Crucifix Run. Run with your arms outstretched to the sides to show that Jesus was crucified on a cross.

Leg 8. Backward Walk. Walk backward with your arms crossed over your chest to show that Jesus died.

Leg 9. Skip. Skip, yelling, "Ta-da!" to show that Jesus came back to life.

Lesson: Place objects in your Easter basket beforehand so that it's ready to show to students.

Ask students, how many of you got an Easter basket this morning?

Did any of your Easter baskets have this grass in the bottom? (Pull out some grass from your basket.) The grass reminds us of the hay that Jesus slept on in the manger when He was born.

Did any of you get any chocolate wrapped up in shiny foil, like Hershey Kisses, or York Peppermint Patties, or Rolos, or Reeses' miniatures? (Pull out your chocolate coins.) When we see shiny wrapping, it reminds us of the 30 shiny coins that the priests gave to Judas so that Judas would tell them where Jesus was so that they could arrest Him.

Did any of you get any roosters or chickens in your Easter basket, like a chocolate rooster, or some Peeps? (Pull out your item.) Chickens and roosters remind us of how Peter said that He didn't know Jesus three times the night Jesus was arrested, and then, a rooster crowed just as Jesus said it would, and Peter felt sorry about saying He didn't know Jesus.

What about your baskets? Did it look like mine with the wood or plastic pieces woven together like this? Our baskets remind us of how the soldiers tied together some thorns and put them on Jesus' head.

Did any of you get plastic eggs with something inside of them? (Show your plastic egg and empty it.) When we take the candy out of our eggs, it reminds us of how Jesus came out of the grave. The egg is like the grave, and the candy is like Jesus, coming out of the grave.

So, our Easter baskets were meant to tell us the story of how Jesus was born, how He died, and how He came back to life on Easter!

Game: Resurrection Race – Divide students into pairs. Have each pair line up along one line. Place cones a good distance from the line, directly in front of the pairs.

Give each pair two rolls of toilet paper. On, "Go!" the first person from each pair will wrap their partner in toilet paper, using the whole roll. The wrapped person will then break free of the toilet paper and run around the cone and back toward their partner. They will then wrap their partner, and the second person will do the same thing. The first pair to have both people wrapped and run around the cone wins.

Explain to students that this is what will happen to us. Our bodies will be dead, but then when Jesus comes back, He will bring our bodies back to life, just like God brought Jesus' body back to life.

Game: Resurrection Tag – Pick one student to be It. That student is Death. Pick another student to be Jesus. When Death tags someone, they fall down and lie on the ground like they're dead. Jesus can then come to tag them, and they can get back up. If Death tags Jesus, Jesus must count to three (because Jesus was dead for three days), but can then get up again. If Jesus tags Death, the round is over. Play until everyone has had a chance to be both Death and Jesus or as long as time permits.

Remind students that Jesus will come back one day and will raise everyone who believes in Him back to life, just as God raised Jesus back to life on Easter morning.

Closing Prayer: Jesus, we thank You for taking our place on the cross and for coming again one day to raise us all up so that we can live forever with You. Amen.

Jesus is Raised!

Use this children's Sunday School lesson to teach kids about Jesus' resurrection on Easter Sunday and our resurrection when He comes again.

Needed: Bibles, toilet paper rolls, cones or another placement marker

Lesson: Read Matthew 27:62-66.)

"The next day, the one after Preparation Day, the chief priests and the Pharisees went to Pilate. 'Sir,' they said, 'we remember that while He was still alive that deceiver said, 'After three days I will rise again.' So give the order for the tomb to be made secure until the third day. Otherwise, His disciples may come and steal the body and tell the people that He has been raised from the dead. This last deception will be worse than the first.'

"'Take a guard,' Pilate answered. 'Go, make the tomb as secure as you know how.' So they went and made the tomb secure by putting a seal on the stone and posting the guard."

On the Saturday after Jesus died, the priests asked Pilate, the Roman governor, to put guards around Jesus' grave. Why does it say that they did that? (The priests didn't want Jesus' followers to come steal Jesus' body and then, lie and tell people that Jesus came back to life.)

(Read Matthew 28:1-10.)

"After the Sabbath, at dawn on the first day of the week, Mary Magdalene and the other Mary went to look at the tomb.

"There was a violent earthquake, for an angel of the Lord came down from heaven and, going to the tomb, rolled back the stone and sat on it. His appearance was like lightning, and his clothes were white as snow. The guards were so afraid of him that they shook and became like dead men.

"The angel said to the women, 'Do not be afraid, for I know that you are looking for Jesus, who was crucified. He is not here; He has risen, just as He said. Come and see the place where He lay. Then go quickly and tell His disciples: "He has risen from the dead and is going ahead of you into Galilee. There you will see Him." Now I have told you.'

"So the women hurried away from the tomb, afraid yet filled with joy, and ran to tell His disciples. Suddenly Jesus met them. 'Greetings,' He said. They came to Him, clasped His feet and worshiped Him. Then Jesus said to them, 'Do not be afraid. Go and tell My brothers to go to Galilee; there they will see Me.'

How did Jesus come back to life? (After Jesus died, God brought Him back to life.)

God can do anything. He can even make dead people come back to life. One day, when Jesus comes back to Earth, He will make our souls go back into our bodies and bring our bodies back to life. Our bodies will be perfect, and we will live forever with Jesus and God forever.

(Read Matthew 28:11-15.)

"While the women were on their way, some of the guards went into the city and reported to the chief priests everything that had happened. When the chief priests had met with the elders and devised a plan, they gave the soldiers a large sum of money, telling them, 'You are to say, "His disciples came during the night and stole Him away while we were asleep." If this report gets to the governor, we will satisfy him and keep you out of trouble.' So the soldiers took the money and did as they were instructed. And this story has been widely circulated among the Jews to this very day."

Why did the priests pay the guards to lie about Jesus being alive again?

The priests didn't want people to believe in Jesus, and they didn't want people to know He came back to life, so they paid the guards to lie about what happened.

Game: Resurrection Race – Divide students into pairs. Have each pair line up along one line. Place cones a good distance from the line, directly in front of the pairs.

Give each pair two rolls of toilet paper. On, "Go!" the first person from each pair will wrap their partner in toilet paper, using the whole roll. The wrapped person will then break free of the toilet paper and run around the cone and back toward their partner. They will then wrap their partner, and the second person will do the same thing. The first pair to have both people wrapped and run around the cone wins.

Explain to students that this is what will happen to us. Our bodies will be dead, but then when Jesus comes back, He will bring our bodies back to life, just like God brought Jesus' body back to life.

Game: Resurrection Tag – Pick one student to be It. That student is Death. Pick another student to be Jesus. When Death tags someone, they fall down and lie on the ground like they're dead. Jesus can then come to tag them, and they can get back up. If Death tags Jesus, Jesus must count to three (because Jesus was dead for three days), but can then get up again. If Jesus tags Death, the round is over. Play until everyone has had a chance to be both Death and Jesus or as long as time permits.

Remind students that Jesus will come back one day and will raise everyone who believes in Him back to life, just as God raised Jesus back to life on Easter morning.

Closing Prayer: Father God, we praise You for bringing Jesus back to life and for promising to raise us again one day. Help us always to believe in You so that we'll be ready when Jesus returns one day. In Jesus' name we pray, amen.

The Empty Grave

Use this children's Sunday School lesson to teach kids about the resurrection of Christ and our resurrection when He comes again.

Needed: Bibles, balloons, a box, three signs saying "Sorry. He's Not Here!", cupcakes for each student with re-lighting candles in them

Intro Game: Don't Let it Fall! – Gather students in a circle. As you toss a balloon up into the air in the middle of the circle, call one of the student's names. That student must run to hit the balloon back into the air before it touches the ground. The student next to them then runs to hit the balloon. The round continues until the balloon hits the floor.

Play as many rounds as you like. The last time the balloon drops (or if it ever pops), announce, "I'm sorry, kids. The balloon has dropped for the last time and now, it's dead. Let's have a funeral for our dear balloon."

Gather the balloon and place it in the box. Say a few words over it and invite others to do the same.

Lesson: Read John 19:38.

"Later, Joseph of Arimathea asked Pilate for the body of Jesus. Now Joseph was a disciple of Jesus, but secretly because he feared the Jewish leaders. With Pilate's permission, he came and took the body away."

It says that Joseph of Arimathea was a disciple of Jesus, but secretly because he was afraid of the Jews. Why do you think he was afraid to tell the Jews that he was a follower of Jesus? (It was against the law to believe in Jesus, so he was afraid that he would be arrested like Jesus was.)

Should he have been afraid to tell people he believed in Jesus? (No.)

We should never be afraid or embarrassed to say that we believe in Jesus. We have to stand up and speak out for Jesus so that other people can believe in Him too and be saved.

(Read John 19:39-20:18.)

"He was accompanied by Nicodemus, the man who earlier had visited Jesus at night. Nicodemus brought a mixture of myrrh and aloes, about seventy-five pounds. Taking Jesus' body, the two of them wrapped it, with the spices, in strips of linen. This was in accordance with Jewish burial customs. At the place where Jesus was crucified, there was a garden, and in the garden a new tomb, in which no one had ever been laid. Because it was the Jewish day of Preparation and since the tomb was nearby, they laid Jesus there.

"Early on the first day of the week, while it was still dark, Mary Magdalene went to the tomb and saw that the stone had been removed from the entrance. So she came running to Simon Peter and the other disciple, the one Jesus loved, and said, 'They have taken the Lord out of the tomb, and we don't know where they have put Him!'

"So Peter and the other disciple started for the tomb. Both were running, but the other disciple outran Peter and reached the tomb first. He bent over and looked in at the strips of linen lying there but did not go in. Then Simon Peter came along behind him and went straight into the tomb. He saw the strips of linen lying there, as well as the cloth that had been wrapped around Jesus' head. The cloth was still lying in its place, separate from the linen. Finally the other disciple, who had reached the tomb first, also went inside. He saw and believed. (They still did not understand from Scripture that Jesus had to rise from the dead.) Then the disciples went back to where they were staying.

"Now Mary stood outside the tomb crying. As she wept, she bent over to look into the tomb and saw two angels in white, seated where Jesus' body had been, one at the head and the other at the foot.

"They asked her, 'Woman, why are you crying?'

"'They have taken my Lord away,' she said, 'and I don't know where they have put Him.' At this, she turned around and saw Jesus standing there, but she did not realize that it was Jesus.

"He asked her, 'Woman, why are you crying? Who is it you are looking for?'

"Thinking He was the gardener, she said, 'Sir, if you have carried Him away, tell me where You have put Him, and I will get Him.'

"Jesus said to her, 'Mary.'

"She turned toward him and cried out in Aramaic, 'Rabboni!' (which means "Teacher").

"Jesus said, 'Do not hold on to Me, for I have not yet ascended to the Father. Go instead to my brothers and tell them, "I am ascending to my Father and your Father, to my God and your God."'

"Mary Magdalene went to the disciples with the news: 'I have seen the Lord!' And she told them that He had said these things to her."

How did Jesus come back to life? (After Jesus died, God brought Him back to life.)

God can do anything. He can even make dead people come back to life. One day, when Jesus comes back to Earth, He will make our souls go back into our bodies and bring our bodies back to life. Our bodies will be perfect, and we will live with Jesus and God forever.

Jesus told Mary that He was going back to God. When had Jesus been with God before?

Jesus was in Heaven with God before He became a human baby. Jesus is part of God Himself.

Now that Jesus' work of teaching us and dying on the cross for us was done, He said He was going back up to Heaven to be with God again. Someday, Jesus is going to come back to Earth to bring us all back from the dead, and we will live with Him and God forever.

Game: Don't Let it Fall! part 2 – Play the intro game again, taking the balloon back out of the box or blowing up a new one. Explain that even though your balloon was dead, it came back to life just like Jesus came back to life and will bring all of us back to life when He comes again.

Activity: Resurrection Hunt – Before class, find three rooms or areas in your church that you can use for this activity. In each room, place a large sign that reads, "Sorry. He's Not Here!"

Say, Wow! What an experience Mary Magdalene, Peter, and John had that morning. Think about it. All three of them went to the tomb and saw that the big rock had been rolled away from the entrance. They looked in and found nothing but the special wrappings that had been around Jesus' body. For a while, all they could imagine was that someone had stolen Jesus' body. Then they wondered, What if He really has come back to life?

Today, you're going hunting for Jesus just as Mary and Peter and John did.

(Take children to visit the rooms you chose earlier. If you're in an area of your church where you will not disturb others, you can let children run ahead once they know which room you're heading to. When you get to each room, ask one child to carry away the sign that reads, "Sorry. He's Not Here!")

(After visiting all the empty rooms, go to where you'll be serving a snack and say:)

How did you feel each time we got to a room and found the sign telling us Jesus wasn't there?

Mary Magdalene, Peter, and John were probably pretty disappointed when they couldn't find Jesus' body.

When we go looking for something and don't find it, we have lots of questions. I'm sure Peter and John wondered what had happened to Jesus' body. But the Bible says that John "saw and believed." That means he knew that Jesus was alive. God wants us to know that Jesus is alive too.

Mary Magdalene, Peter, and John eventually did see Jesus. They found what they were looking for. So, since you all did such a great job looking too, I have something for you.

(Give each student a cupcake with a trick candle in it. Light the candles and have students try to blow them out.)

What happened to the candles? (They kept lighting back up.)

That's kind of what happened on Easter morning. People thought they had gotten rid Jesus, just as you thought you had blown out your candles. But God had other plans. God brought Jesus back to life, just like your candles kept lighting back up.

Closing Prayer: Father God, we thank You for bringing Jesus back to life. And we thank You that You're going to bring us back to life one day too. Help us to keep believing in You until that day happens. In Jesus' name we pray, amen.

On the Road to Emmaus

Use this children's Sunday School lesson to teach kids about how Jesus fulfills prophecy from the Old Testament.

Needed: Bibles, slips of paper with prophetic statements about Jesus written on them, close-up images of common objects, drawing paper, crayons or colored pencils

> https://brightside.me/wonder-quizzes/test-can-you-recognize-everyday-objects-close-up-262360/

Intro Game #1: Fulfilling Prophecy – Print or write out prophecy clues about Jesus, along with their Scripture reference, on strips of paper and hide them around the room. Kids rush to find them and then, put them in order according to book of the Bible.

When they're finished, explain that all of the statements are prophecies about one person and see if they know who the prophecies are describing.

Prophecies could include:

Will be born in Bethlehem – Micah 5:2
Will not have a human father – Isaiah 7:14
Will be a prophet – Deuteronomy 18:15
Will be protected by angels – Psalm 91:10-12
Will ride a donkey into Jerusalem – Zechariah 9:9
Will be rejected by people – Isaiah 53:1-3
Will be betrayed by a friend – Psalm 41:9
Will be betrayed for 30 pieces of silver – Zechariah 11:12-13
Will die for other people's sins – Isaiah 53:8
Will come back from the dead – Psalm 16:10

Intro Game #2 – What is It? – Show kids close-up images of everyday objects and let them guess what the images are.

Play until interest fades. Then, explain that it's difficult to tell what something is sometimes.

Lesson: Tell students, Today's story happened the same day that Jesus rose from the dead.

(Read Luke 24:13-16.)

"Now that same day two of them were going to a village called Emmaus, about seven miles from Jerusalem. They were talking with each other about everything that had happened. As they talked and discussed these things with each other, Jesus himself came up and walked along with them; but they were kept from recognizing Him.

Jesus was talking with the two disciples as they walked on the road, but it says that they were kept from recognizing Him. They didn't know who He was. How do you think they were kept from recognizing Him?

God made them think they were seeing somebody else other than Jesus.

(Read Luke 24:17-27.)

"He asked them, 'What are you discussing together as you walk along?'

"They stood still, their faces downcast. One of them, named Cleopas, asked Him, 'Are You the only one visiting Jerusalem who does not know the things that have happened there in these days?'

"'What things?' He asked.

"'About Jesus of Nazareth,' they replied. 'He was a prophet, powerful in word and deed before God and all the people. The chief priests and our rulers handed Him over to be sentenced to death, and they crucified Him; but we had hoped that He was the one who was going to redeem Israel. And what is more, it is the third day since all this took place. In addition, some of our women amazed us. They went to the tomb early this morning but didn't find His body. They came and told us that they had seen a vision of angels, who said He was alive. Then some of our companions went to the tomb and found it just as the women had said, but they did not see Jesus.'

"He said to them, 'How foolish you are, and how slow to believe all that the prophets have spoken! Did not the Messiah have to suffer these things and then enter His glory?' And beginning with Moses and all the Prophets, He explained to them what was said in all the Scriptures concerning Himself."

Jesus said that the Christ had to put to death and rise again. Then, He explained it to them in the books of Moses and the books of the prophets. What are the books of Moses and the books of the prophets? Do we still have those books? Can we read them? (Yes, they're the books of the Old Testament in the Bible.)

Jesus is saying that the books of the Old Testament prophesied about Him, telling the future about Him and what He was going to do. How could Moses and the prophets have known what was going to happen to Jesus before Jesus was even born? (God told them about Jesus and what He was going to do.)

It was God's plan for Jesus to come and die in our place so that we could be forgiven for our sins and so that we could go to Heaven when we die instead of going to Hell.

Why do you think God told the writers Moses and the prophets about Jesus before He even came?

God told the writers of the Old Testament about Jesus so that people would know He was the chosen one when He came. They would see Him fulfilling the prophecies and know that He was the one God wanted us to believe in.

It was like God was saying, "When you see someone who matches all these prophecies I gave you, that's the one I want you to believe in." The prophecies are God's clues to us to believe in Jesus.

(Read Luke 24:28-31.)

"As they approached the village to which they were going, Jesus continued on as if He were going farther. But they urged Him strongly, 'Stay with us, for it is nearly evening; the day is almost over.' So He went in to stay with them.

"When He was at the table with them, He took bread, gave thanks, broke it and began to give it to them. Then their eyes were opened and they recognized Him, and He disappeared from their sight."

It says that the two disciples finally realized it was Jesus talking to them when He took some bread, gave thanks, broke it, and gave it to them. Why would Jesus doing that remind them of Jesus and make them realize that it was Jesus talking to them?

Jesus had done the same thing a few nights before this when He started the tradition of Communion. He had taken the bread, given thanks, broke it, and handed it to His disciples, saying "Take and eat. This is My body, which is broken for you." The bread being broken reminds us of how Jesus' body was hurt when He was being crucified.

Craft: Drawing Prophecy – Show kids the slips of paper from the Fulfilling Prophecy game. Give them drawing supplies and have them draw one scene from one of the prophecies. Then, remind students that God told the prophets that Jesus would do each of those things hundreds or even thousands of year before Jesus was born.

Closing Prayer: Father God, thank You for telling the writers of the Bible about Jesus before He was born so that we could see how You planned to send Him to earth to save us. Help us to believe in Him and to believe in You even more because we know that You had a plan for Jesus, and You have a plan for the future too. In Jesus' name we pray, amen.

Recommended Extra

Jesus Walks with Two Friends – free coloring and activity pages

https://freesundayschoolcurriculum.weebly.com/uploads/1/2/5/0/12503916/lesson_74_jesus_walks_with_two_friends.pdf

Jesus Appears to His Disciples

Use this children's Sunday School lesson to teach students about faith and how Jesus appeared to the doubting disciple.

Needed: Bibles, a list of statements for a true/false game

Intro Game: The Unbelievable – Divide students into two teams. You'll read a list of statements, and they have to vote as a team whether they believe each of your statements or not. The team with the most correct answers wins.

Here are some statements all about animals.

> https://www.womansday.com/life/pet-care/a3900/animal-facts-for-kids-true-or-false-78075/

For more general questions, try these.

1. Yogurt is made with bacteria. (True. Bacteria ferment the milk.)

2. Your ears help keep you balanced. (True. The fluid in your ears gives you a sense of balance.)

3. Zebras are the fastest land animal in the world. (False. Cheetahs are the fastest.)

4. A snake's skin feels slimy. (False. It feels dry.)

5. Adult people have 502 bones in their body. (False. Most people only have 206 bones.)

6. DNA stands for 'Deoxyribonucleic acid.' (True.)

7. Crocodiles do not sweat, so they breathe through their mouth to cool down. (True.)

8. The Grand Canyon is the deepest place on earth. (False. The Mariana Trench is the deepest place we know of.)

9. Humans have been to every planet in our solar system. (False. We've only been to the moon so far.)

10. Jesus was dead for three days but came back to life. (True. God did a miracle to bring Jesus back to life.)

Explain that today's story is about one of the disciples who didn't believe that Jesus came back from the dead.

Lesson: Explain to students that this happened the same day Jesus rose from the dead on Easter morning.

(Read John 20:19.)

"On the evening of that first day of the week, when the disciples were together, with the doors locked for fear of the Jewish leaders, Jesus came and stood among them and said, 'Peace be with you!'"

The disciples were in the house together with the door locked. How did Jesus come in? He didn't knock.

Jesus can come to be with us wherever we are. He doesn't need to go through doors or windows anymore.

(Read John 20:20.)

"After He said this, He showed them His hands and side. The disciples were overjoyed when they saw the Lord."

Why would Jesus show them His hands and side?

He was showing them the nail holes in His hands and the hole in His side where the soldier stabbed Him with a spear, so that they would know it was really Him.

(Read John 20:21.)

"Again Jesus said, 'Peace be with you! As the Father has sent Me, I am sending you.'"

Jesus said, "As the Father sent Me, so I send you." What did God the Father send Jesus to do? (God sent Jesus to tell other people about God and to die on the cross so that we could be saved.)

What is Jesus sending us to do? (To tell other people about God and Jesus so that they can be saved too.)

(Read John 20:22.)

"And with that He breathed on them and said, 'Receive the Holy Spirit.'"

What happened when Jesus breathed on the disciples? (The Holy Spirit came to live inside them.)

What is the Holy Spirit?

The Holy Spirit is the part of God and Jesus that lives in our hearts and is always with us.

(Read John 20:23-28.)

"'If you forgive anyone's sins, their sins are forgiven; if you do not forgive them, they are not forgiven.'

"Now Thomas (also known as Didymus), one of the Twelve, was not with the disciples when Jesus came. So the other disciples told him, 'We have seen the Lord!'

"But he said to them, 'Unless I see the nail marks in His hands and put my finger where the nails were, and put my hand into His side, I will not believe.'

"A week later His disciples were in the house again, and Thomas was with them. Though the doors were locked, Jesus came and stood among them and said, 'Peace be with you!' Then He said to Thomas, 'Put your finger here; see my hands. Reach out your hand and put it into My side. Stop doubting and believe.'

"Thomas said to Him, 'My Lord and my God!'"

Why did Thomas call Jesus "Lord and God"? Isn't there only one God?

Jesus is part of God. There are three parts of the one God; God the Father, Jesus, and the Holy Spirit. God has three parts, just like we have three parts. Our three parts are our body, our heart (which is our emotions and mind), and our soul or spirit.

(Read John 20:29.)

"Then Jesus told him, 'Because you have seen Me, you have believed; blessed are those who have not seen and yet have believed.'"

Jesus said that there would be people who never saw Him but who will believe He rose from the dead and that those people will be blessed, or rewarded, by God because they believe in Jesus. Who are those people that Jesus is talking about? (Us!)

We've never seen Jesus, but we still believe in Him, and God will reward us for that by letting us go to Heaven when we die.

Game: Trust Fall – Have students pair up. One student stands behind the other. The student in front closes their eyes and falls back, trusting the one behind them to catch them. Then the partners switch roles.

Let each pair try the activity a couple of times, getting more and more comfortable. Then, ask, Was it difficult to have faith that your partner would catch you?

Could you see them behind you when you closed your eyes and let yourself fall back?

That's how much faith God wants us to have in Him. Even though we've never seen Jesus, we need to have faith in Him.

Game: Disciple Tag – Choose one student to be It. When they tag someone, that person links hands with them and joins their team. They continue adding people to their team, linking hands with each one until all but one student is part of their chain. That remaining student becomes It for the next round.

Play two or three rounds and then, explain that when we tell people about Jesus, we want them to believe in Jesus too. If they do, they become a Christian and join our team. Then, they help us tell more people about Jesus.

Closing Prayer: Jesus, we thank You for coming to tell us about God and for dying on the cross to take the punishment for our sin. Now, we pray that You'll help us to have faith in You so that we live forever with You. Amen.

Recommended Extra

Jesus Shows His Hands and Feet – free coloring and activity pages

https://freesundayschoolcurriculum.weebly.com/uploads/1/2/5/0/12503916/lesson_75_jesus_shows_his_hands_and_feet.pdf

Jesus Forgives Peter

Use this children's Sunday School lesson to teach kids how important it is to love Jesus.

Needed: Bibles, drawing paper, crayons or colored pencils

Lesson: Explain that this story probably happened a couple of weeks after Jesus rose from the dead.

(Read John 21:1-6.)

"Afterward Jesus appeared again to His disciples, by the Sea of Galilee. It happened this way: Simon Peter, Thomas (also known as Didymus), Nathanael from Cana in Galilee, the sons of Zebedee, and two other disciples were together. 'I'm going out to fish,' Simon Peter told them, and they said, 'We'll go with you.' So they went out and got into the boat, but that night they caught nothing.

"Early in the morning, Jesus stood on the shore, but the disciples did not realize that it was Jesus.

"He called out to them, 'Friends, haven't you any fish?'

"'No,' they answered.

"He said, 'Throw your net on the right side of the boat and you will find some.' When they did, they were unable to haul the net in because of the large number of fish."

Why did the disciples not catch anything, but then, caught a lot when Jesus told them to try the other side?

Sometimes, when we try to do things on our own, it doesn't work out the way we want. But if we listen to what Jesus tells us to do, He will help us.

(Read John 21:7.)

"Then the disciple whom Jesus loved said to Peter, 'It is the Lord!' As soon as Simon Peter heard him say, 'It is the Lord,' he wrapped his outer garment around him (for he had taken it off) and jumped into the water."

Why did Peter jump out of the boat when he realized it was Jesus on the beach, instead of waiting for the boat to get back to shore? (Peter was so excited to see Jesus that he didn't want to wait.)

Are you excited to see Jesus?

Someday, we will see Jesus, either when we die and go to Heaven or when Jesus comes back from Heaven. Then, we'll be with Jesus all the time. But even before we see Him, we can still be excited to spend time with Jesus now. What are some things we can do to spend time with Jesus now? (We can spend time with Jesus by praying, reading our Bible, going to church, etc.)

Let's spend some time Jesus right now.

Prayer Activity: Spending Time with Jesus – Have students separate around the room. Ask them to spend 5 minutes praying to Jesus. Tell them that they can talk to Jesus about anything they want to. After 4 minutes, ask them to stop talking to Jesus and to listen to anything He might want to say to them in their heart.

Lesson Continues: Read John 21:8-14.

"The other disciples followed in the boat, towing the net full of fish, for they were not far from shore, about a hundred yards. When they landed, they saw a fire of burning coals there with fish on it, and some bread.

"Jesus said to them, 'Bring some of the fish you have just caught.' So Simon Peter climbed back into the boat and dragged the net ashore. It was full of large fish, 153, but even with so many the net was not torn. Jesus said to them, 'Come and have breakfast.' None of the disciples dared ask Him, 'Who are you?' They knew it was the Lord. Jesus came, took the bread and gave it to them, and did the same with the fish. This was now the third time Jesus appeared to His disciples after He was raised from the dead."

Do you remember how when Jesus was arrested, Peter told the guards three times that He didn't know Jesus? He said he didn't know Jesus because he was afraid that the guards would arrest him like they arrested Jesus. But now listen to what Jesus does.

(Read John 21:15-17.)

"When they had finished eating, Jesus said to Simon Peter, 'Simon son of John, do you love Me more than these?'

"'Yes, Lord,' he said, 'you know that I love You.'

"Jesus said, 'Feed My lambs.'

"Again Jesus said, 'Simon son of John, do you love Me?'

"He answered, 'Yes, Lord, you know that I love You.'

"Jesus said, 'Take care of My sheep.'

"The third time He said to him, 'Simon son of John, do you love Me?'

"Peter was hurt because Jesus asked him the third time, 'Do you love me?' He said, 'Lord, You know all things; You know that I love You.'

"Jesus said, 'Feed My sheep.'"

Why did Jesus ask Peter three times if he loved Him? (Because Peter had said that He didn't know Jesus three times the night Jesus was arrested.)

Why does Jesus ask if Peter loves Him instead of asking him something else? (The thing that Jesus cares about most is if we love Him.) Do you love Jesus?

And what did Jesus ask Peter to do? (Feed and take care of His sheep.)

Did Jesus have sheep? What is He talking about?

Jesus is telling Peter to take care of Jesus' followers. And one way we take care of people is to help them.

Craft: Servant Brainstorming – Give students drawing supplies and have them draw a picture of one thing they can do this week to help someone else. When everyone is finished, have them share their drawings and ideas. Remind students that Jesus told Peter, and He tells us, to take care of His people.

Game: Sword Drill – Give each student a Bible and say, Jesus also told Peter to feed His sheep. That means He wanted Peter to teach His people God's Word. But if we want to teach other people, we have to know the Bible, don't we? We have to read it so that we know what it says.

Let's practice getting to know our Bible so that we can help teach other people. Call out the name of one of the books of the Bible. The student who finds that book first wins. To make it a little more difficult, you can call out the chapter and verse of a book or the name of a Biblical person or event.

Closing Prayer: Jesus, we thank You for forgiving Peter when He said He didn't know and we thank You for forgiving us of our sins too. Help us to love You our whole lives and to teach other people about You. Amen.

Jesus Gives His Disciples Their Mission and Promises to Always be With Them

Use this children's Sunday School lesson to teach kids about the Great Commission.

Needed: Bibles, balloons

Intro Game: Disciple Tag – Choose one student to be It. When they tag someone, that person links hands with them and joins their team. They continue adding people to their team, linking hands with each one until all but one student is part of their chain. That remaining student becomes It for the next round.

Play two or three rounds and then, explain that when we tell people about Jesus, we want them to believe in Jesus too. If they do, they become a Christian and join our team. Then, they help us tell more people about Jesus.

Lesson: Explain that this story happened a few weeks after Jesus rose from the dead.

(Read Matthew 28:16-18.)

"Then the eleven disciples went to Galilee, to the mountain where Jesus had told them to go. When they saw Him, they worshiped Him; but some doubted. Then Jesus came to them and said, 'All authority in heaven and on earth has been given to Me.'"

Jesus said that all power in Heaven and Earth had been given to Him. Who gave Him that power? (God.)

God gave Jesus that power because Jesus did everything God wanted Him to do. Jesus never, ever, in His whole life did anything wrong, and then, Jesus died as a punishment for our sins to save us. So, God gave Him all the power.

(Read Matthew 28:19-20.)

"'Therefore go and make disciples of all nations, baptizing them in the name of the Father and of the Son and of the Holy Spirit, and teaching them to obey everything I have commanded you. And surely I am with you always, to the very end of the age.'"

What did Jesus tell the disciples to do? (He told them to go make new disciples for Jesus and to baptize them.)

And that's still what Jesus wants us to do. He wants us to tell other people about Jesus and God so that they can be Jesus' disciples too and go to Heaven when they die.

How long did Jesus say He would be with us? (Until the end of the age.)

That means that until the end of the world, Jesus will be with us.

How is Jesus with us if He isn't here on Earth anymore? (Jesus is with us because He lives in our hearts through the Holy Spirit if we believe in Him.)

Demonstration: Jesus is With Us! – Give each student a balloon. Tell them to blow it up but not tie it.

Ask, What's inside your balloon? (Air.)

How do you know that? You can't see it. How do you know it's there?

You see what the air does, don't you? You see the balloon filling up, so you know there's air in the there.

The Holy Spirit is like air. He's a Spirit, which means He's invisible, just like air is invisible. But we know that Jesus is still with us through the Holy Spirit, even if we can't see Him, because we can feel Him living in our hearts. We can feel Him teaching us and helping us to be better. Jesus will always be with us in our hearts through the Holy Spirit if we believe in Him.

Activity: Acting It Out – Divide students into groups of two or three. Have each group decide on and act out a conversation in which someone tells another person about Jesus and invites them to come to church or a church event.

Game: Disciple Tag – Play the intro game again.

Closing Prayer: Jesus, thank You for sending the Holy Spirit to live in our hearts so that You will always be with us. We pray that You'll help us to tell other people about You so that they can be Your followers too and live with You forever. Amen.

Recommended Extra

Delivering the Invitation – free object lesson, along with free coloring and activity pages

> https://www.sermons4kids.com/delivering-invitation.html

Jesus Goes Back Up to Heaven – The Ascension

Use this children's Sunday School lesson to tell students about how Jesus went back up to Heaven and what will happen when He returns

Needed: Bibles, various objects, drawing paper, crayons or colored pencils

Intro Game: What's Missing? – Have students close their eyes. While their eyes are closed, take something from the room and put it outside the door where the students can't see it. Tell the students to open their eyes and guess what you took. The first person to guess right gets to remove the next thing.

At the end of the game, bring the objects back into the room and say, Just like we're bringing these things back into our room, so Jesus will come back to Earth one day.

Lesson: Ask students, How did Jesus die? (He died on the cross.)

Did Jesus stay dead? (No, He came back to life after three days.)

(Read Acts 1:1-11 or summarize it with the following story.)

Summary Story: The Bible tells us that Jesus stayed on Earth for 40 days after God raised Him from the dead. During that time, He talked with His disciples, proving to them that He really was alive, and kept teaching them about God and His Kingdom.

When it was almost to the end of the 40 days, Jesus was eating with His disciples, and He said, "Don't leave Jerusalem until you receive the Holy Spirit. He is a gift that God promised to give you, and you've heard Me talk about Him. He's going to come to you in just a few more days."

His disciples asked Him, "Are you going to kick the Romans out of Israel and give us back our country now? We're tired of having the Romans rule over us."

But Jesus said, "You don't need to know when God is going to give you back your kingdom. Just wait until the Holy Spirit comes down. He will give you power so that you will be able to tell everyone about Me. I want you to tell the people in this country and the people all over the world all the things I taught you about God and about how I died and took the punishment for their sins so that they could be forgiven."

After Jesus said this, He floated up into the sky. He floated so high that He went into the clouds, and the disciples couldn't see Him anywhere.

They were still looking up into the sky when suddenly, two angels appeared beside them. They said, "Men, why are you looking up into the sky? Jesus, who you just saw being taken up into Heaven, will come back down from Heaven someday."

Review and Discussion Questions
Who did Jesus say was going to come down and give the disciples power? (The Holy Spirit.)

What does the Holy Spirit do?

The Holy Spirit lives inside everyone who believes in Jesus. He's the part of God that teaches us the right things to do and tells us not to do the wrong things. He also makes us brave to tell other people about Jesus and helps us to know what to say to people when we try to tell them about Jesus.

Jesus went up in the clouds. Where do you think He was going? (Heaven.)

Jesus was going back to Heaven to be with God. Jesus lived in Heaven with God before He was born as a human baby. Because His work of teaching us and dying for us on the cross was over, Jesus went back to Heaven.

The angels said that Jesus would come back again someday. Why do you think Jesus is going to come back?

Jesus is going to do a lot of things when He comes back, but mainly He's coming to make this world a better place.

Have any of you ever known somebody who died?

When Jesus comes back, He will bring everyone who believes in Him back to life, and they will die ever again.

Have any of you ever been sick?

When Jesus comes back, He will make our bodies so healthy that none of us will ever get sick again.

Have any of you ever been sad about something?

When Jesus comes back, no one will ever be sad again because Jesus will make it so that nothing bad ever happens again.

Have any of you ever had someone do something wrong to you? Or have any of you ever done anything that was wrong?

We've all done things that were wrong. We've all broken the rules and had other people do wrong things to us. But when Jesus comes back, no one will ever do anything wrong again. Jesus will put the devil in Hell forever, and He will make us to be perfect so that no one will do anything wrong ever again.

What are some of your favorite animals?

Does anyone like lions or cobra snakes or other dangerous animals?

Can you pet those dangerous animals?

When Jesus comes back, all the animals will be nice. They'll all eat plants and not hunt each other. We'll eat plants only, too, and not eat the animals. And you'll be able to go up and pet your favorite animals. Even if they're dangerous now, Jesus will make it so that they're nice when He comes back.

And Jesus will do one more thing when He comes back. I said that He will send the devil to Hell forever. He will also send everyone who doesn't believe in God to Hell. That's why we have to do our best to make sure we're doing what God wants and telling other people about Him so that they can live with Jesus and not go to Hell.

Craft: Jesus' Return – Give students drawing supplies and have them draw a picture of what they think it will be like when Jesus comes back to Earth. Remind them that He will change us so that we won't die or get sick or be sad or do anything wrong. Everyone and all the animals will be at peace.

When they're finished with their drawings, have them explain them to the class.

Game: Disciple Tag – Choose one student to be It. When they tag someone, that person links hands with them and joins their team. They continue adding people to their team, linking hands with each one until all but one student is part of their chain. That remaining student becomes It for the next round.

Play two or three rounds and then, explain that when we tell people about Jesus, we want them to believe in Jesus too. If they do, they become a Christian and join our team. Then, they help us tell more people about Jesus.

Alternative Game: Resurrection Tag – Pick one student to be It. That student is Death. Pick another student to be Jesus. When Death tags someone, they fall down and lie on the ground like they're dead. Jesus can then come to tag them, and they can get back up. If Death tags Jesus, Jesus must count to three (because Jesus was dead for three days), but can then get up again. If Jesus tags Death, the round is over. Play until everyone has had a chance to be both Death and Jesus or as long as time permits.

Remind students that Jesus will come back one day and will raise everyone who believes in Him back to life.

Closing Prayer: Jesus, we thank You for coming to teach us and to die on the cross to take the punishment for our sins. Help us to believe in You until You come back and make the world the way it's supposed to be. Amen.

Recommended Extra

Jesus Goes Back to Heaven – free coloring and activity pages

> https://freesundayschoolcurriculum.weebly.com/uploads/1/2/5/0/12503916/lesson_76_jesus_goes_back_to_heaven.pdf

Made in the USA
Monee, IL
04 February 2024